FOOD LOVERS

ONE POT

FOOD LOVERS

ONE POT

RECIPES SELECTED BY MARIKA KUCEROVA

Trans
Atlantic
Press

All recipes serve four people, unless otherwise indicated.

For best results when cooking the recipes in this book, buy fresh ingredients and follow the instructions carefully. Make sure that everything is properly cooked through before serving, particularly any meat and shellfish, and note that as a general rule vulnerable groups such as the very young, elderly people, pregnant women, convalescents and anyone suffering from an illness should avoid dishes that contain raw or lightly cooked eggs.

For all recipes, quantities are given in standard U.S. cups and imperial measures, followed by the metric equivalent. Follow one set or the other, but not a mixture of both because conversions may not be exact. Standard spoon and cup measurements are level and are based on the following:

1 tsp. = 5 ml, 1 tbsp. = 15 ml, 1 cup = 250 ml / 8 fl oz.

Note that Australian standard tablespoons are 20 ml, so Australian readers should use 3 tsp. in place of 1 tbsp. when measuring small quantities.

The electric oven temperatures in this book are given for conventional ovens with top and bottom heat. When using a fan oven, the temperature should be decreased by about 20–40°F / 10–20°C – check the oven manufacturer's instruction book for further guidance. The cooking times given should be used as an approximate guideline only.

CONTENTS

GREEK STIFADO
(Beef with Onion and Tomato) 6

FISH CASSEROLE with TOMATOES 8

RATATOUILLE 10

SPICY PORK RAGOUT 12

SALMON and LEEK SOUP 14

RATATOUILLE with CHICKEN 16

BRAISED BEEF POT ROAST
with VEGETABLES 18

LAMB STEW with SAFFRON 20

BAKED FISH with VEGETABLES 22

BEEF GOULASH 24

CHICKPEA and BEAN DAL
with CARAWAY POTATOES 26

BEEF RAGOUT with OLIVES 28

BEAN SOUP with PASTA 30

BRAZILIAN SHRIMP STEW
with COCONUT MILK 32

CHICKEN And CHORIZO CHILI 34

TOAD IN THE HOLE
(Sausages in Batter) 36

LANCASHIRE HOTPOT 38

CHEESE-STUFFED TOMATOES 40

CHICKEN STEW with CHANTERELLES 42

LAMB STEW with PEAS and POTATOES 44

BRAISED PORK with MUSHROOMS
and OLIVES 46

BRAISED CHICKEN with VEGETABLES 48

BUTTERNUT SQUASH
and POTATO GRATIN 50

POT AU FEU
(French Chicken and Vegetable Stew) 52

VEAL CASSEROLE with MUSHROOMS
and VEGETABLES 54

BEEF RAGOUT with CHANTERELLE
MUSHROOMS 56

BAKED COD and SEAFOOD COBBLER 58

IRISH STEW with SAVOY CABBAGE 60

CHORIZO STEW with CRÈME FRAÎCHE 62

PAELLA 64

SPICY LAMB with PAPRIKA 66

SPICY CLAM, PORK and
TOMATO STEW 68

CHILI BEEF with WINTER VEGETABLES 70

SHRIMP CREOLE 72

CHUNKY THREE BEAN CHILI 74

SAFFRON RISOTTO with
GREEN ASPARAGUS 76

POTATO GOULASH with SAUERKRAUT 78

BOILED BEEF with VEGETABLES 80

CASSOULET with KNUCKLE OF PORK 82

POT-AU-FEU with BELLY PORK 84

BAKED STUFFED MUSHROOMS with
BACON and CHEESE TOPPING 86

JALFREZI
(Anglo-Indian Curry) 88

FISH STEW with CRÈME FRAÎCHE 90

BEEF and VEGETABLE STEW 92

LAMB STEW with DUMPLINGS 94

GREEK STIFADO (BEEF WITH ONION AND TOMATO)

Ingredients

2¼ lbs / 1 kg beef, from the leg, without bones

6 tbsp. olive oil

salt & freshly milled pepper

2 cloves garlic

3 bay leaves

1 cinnamon stick

½ tsp. nutmeg, grated

½ tsp. cinnamon, ground

½ tsp. cumin, ground

2 tbsp. tomato concentrate or passata

3 tbsp. red wine vinegar

1½ cups / 250 g tomato paste (purée)

2 cups / 500 ml water

scant ½ cup / 100 ml red wine

about 2 lb / 1 kg small onions

14 oz / 400 g small tomatoes

2 tbsp. chopped parsley

Method

Prep and cook time: 2 h 20 min

1 Cut the beef into about 1 inch (2 cm) cubes.

2 Heat the oil in a flameproof casserole and fry the meat until browned on all sides, a few pieces at a time. Season with salt and pepper then take out of the casserole.

3 Peel and finely chop the garlic. Add the garlic, bay leaves, cinnamon stick, nutmeg, cinnamon, cumin and tomato concentrate or passata and sauté, stirring continually.

4 Put the meat back in the casserole and stir. Pour in the red wine vinegar and simmer for 2–3 minutes.

5 Now add the tomato paste (purée) and the water (the meat should be just about covered). Pour in the wine, cover with a lid and simmer for 1 hour.

6 Drop the onions into boiling water and leave for about 1 minute. Drain, put under cold water and peel. Put the onions in the casserole and simmer for another 1 hour.

7 Put the tomatoes in hot water for a few seconds, then immediately into cold water and peel.

8 Put the tomatoes in the casserole about 5 minutes before the end of cooking time. Season to taste and stir in the chopped parsley.

FISH CASSEROLE WITH TOMATOES

Ingredients

1½ lb / 700 g sea bream fillets

salt & freshly milled pepper

2 tbsp. lemon juice

7 oz / 200 g carrots

1 onion

2 tbsp. / 25 g butter

1 bay leaf

1 can chopped tomatoes
(about 14 oz / 400 g)

1¾ cups / 400 ml vegetable broth
(stock)

2 tbsp. small capers

1 tsp. thyme leaves

Method

Prep and cook time: 25 min

1 Cut the fish fillets into bite-size pieces. Season with salt and pepper and drizzle lemon juice over the top.

2 Peel the carrots and chop.

3 Peel the onion and finely chop. Fry in a little butter until soft.

4 Add the bay leaf and the carrots and sauté.

5 Add the tomatoes and pour in the vegetable broth (stock). Season with salt and pepper, cover and simmer for about 10 minutes.

6 Now add the fish and simmer for about 4 minutes until cooked.

7 Stir in the capers, sprinkle thyme leaves over the top and serve.

RATATOUILLE

Ingredients

2 large zucchini (courgettes)

1 large eggplant (aubergine)

1 red bell pepper

1 yellow bell pepper

14 oz / 400 g tomatoes, fresh or canned

1 red onion

4 cloves garlic

3 sprigs fresh thyme

6 tbsp. olive oil

salt & freshly milled pepper

2 tbsp. fresh basil, finely chopped

Method

Prep and cook time: 40 min

1 Trim the zucchini (courgettes) and the eggplant (aubergine). Trim, halve and de-seed the bell peppers.

2 Cut the prepared vegetables into bite-size cubes.

3 If using fresh tomatoes, drop them into boiling water for a few seconds, then immediately into cold water. Now skin the tomatoes, then quarter, de-seed and dice.

4 Peel and finely chop the garlic and the onion. Chop the thyme leaves.

5 Heat 4 tablespoons of oil in a saucepan and fry the diced eggplant over a medium heat for about 2 minutes, stirring continually.

6 Add the zucchini, bell peppers, onion, garlic, thyme and the remaining oil and fry briefly.

7 Now add the tomatoes and season the vegetables to taste with salt and pepper. Cover and simmer over a low heat for about 20 minutes, stirring occasionally.

8 Season with salt and pepper and mix in the basil.

SPICY PORK RAGOUT

Ingredients

1¾ lb / 800 g pork neck, cut into bite-size cubes

1 large white onion

3 cloves garlic

1 stick celery

1 carrot

14 oz / 500 g tomatoes, fresh or canned

4 tbsp. olive oil

¾–1 cup / 200 ml red wine

1 tbsp. tomato paste (purée)

1 tbsp. finely chopped parsley

2 tsp. sugar

salt & freshly milled pepper

¾–1 cup / 200 ml vegetable broth (stock)

½ tsp. cayenne pepper

1 tsp. paprika

fresh oregano, to garnish (optional)

Method

Prep and cook time: 2 h 15 min

1 Peel and finely chop the onion and garlic. Peel the carrot. Chop the carrot and the celery as finely as possible.

2 If using fresh tomatoes, drop them into boiling water for a few seconds, then immediately into cold water. Now skin the tomatoes, then quarter, de-seed and dice.

3 Heat the olive oil in a stew pot and quickly brown the meat on all sides. Take out and set aside.

4 Then in the same oil, sweat the onion, celery, carrot and garlic over a medium heat. Add the meat, sweat briefly with the vegetables, then pour in the red wine.

5 Cook until the wine has evaporated slightly, then stir in the tomatoes and tomato paste (purée). Add the parsley, season with salt and pepper and add the sugar.

6 Bring to a boil, then add the vegetable broth (stock) and simmer over a low heat for about 2 hours.

7 15 minutes before the end of cooking time, stir in the cayenne pepper and paprika. Check the seasoning and add a little more salt and pepper to taste.

8 If the ragout becomes too dry while cooking, stir in 1–2 tablespoons of water. Garnish with oregano, if using.

SALMON AND LEEK SOUP

Ingredients

14 oz / 400 g salmon fillet

2 leeks

1 lb / 450 g potatoes, floury

2 tbsp. / 25 g butter

salt & freshly milled pepper

grated nutmeg

3 cups / 800 ml vegetable broth (stock)

1 tbsp. dill, finely chopped

scant ½ cup / 100 ml cream

lemon juice

flat leaf parsley leaves, to garnish

Method
Prep and cook time: 40 min

1 Slice the leeks into rings.

2 Peel the potatoes and chop into small cubes.

3 Sauté the leek and the potatoes in a little butter and season with salt, pepper and nutmeg.

4 Pour in the vegetable broth (stock), bring to a boil, then simmer for about 20 minutes.

5 Add the dill to the broth (stock) and pour in the cream.

6 Bring to a boil, then add the salmon and simmer gently for about 4–5 minutes until the salmon is opaque in the center. Do not boil.

7 Season to taste with salt, pepper and lemon juice. Ladle into bowls, garnish with the parsley leaves and serve.

RATATOUILLE WITH CHICKEN

Ingredients

1 whole chicken, about 3 lb / 1.25kg
(or chicken pieces)

1 eggplant (aubergine)

2 zucchini (courgettes)

salt

2 red onions

4 tomatoes

1 red bell pepper

2 cloves garlic

salt & freshly milled pepper

olive oil

1 tsp. tomato paste (purée)

1 tsp. paprika

¾–1 cup / about 200 ml chicken broth
(stock)

fresh basil leaves, to garnish

Method
Prep and cook time: 1 h 15 min

1 Heat the oven to 350°F (180°C / gas mark 4).

2 Divide the chicken into eight pieces.

3 Trim the eggplant (aubergine) and the zucchini (courgettes). Chop the eggplant in half lengthways and slice thickly. Cut the zucchini diagonally into thick slices.

4 Peel the onions and cut into wedges. Halve and de-seed the bell peppers and chop. Peel the garlic and cut in half.

5 Season the chicken pieces with salt and pepper and fry in hot oil in a flameproof casserole until golden brown. Remove and set aside.

6 Fry the onion, eggplant and zucchini. Sauté the bell peppers and the garlic, then add the tomato paste (purée) and pour in the broth (stock). Add the tomatoes and paprika and salt and pepper to taste.

7 Put the chicken pieces on top, skin side up and place in the oven for 30–40 minutes. Pour a little broth (stock) over the chicken from time to time and stir.

8 Adjust the seasoning with salt and pepper, sprinkle some basil leaves over the top and serve.

BRAISED BEEF POT ROAST WITH VEGETABLES

Ingredients

2¼ lb / 1 kg beef

2 fennel bulbs

2 celery sticks

2 onions

2 carrots

2 parsley roots (if available)

salt & freshly milled pepper

4 tbsp. oil

2 oz/ 50 g bacon, diced

2 cups / 500 ml beef broth (stock)

3–4 allspice berries, crushed

10 peppercorns, crushed

2 bay leaves

Method

Prep and cook time: 3 h

1 Remove any tough outer layers from the fennel bulbs and the core and slice thinly.

2 Cut the celery diagonally into pieces.

3 Peel the onions, the carrots and the parsley roots and chop.

4 Season the beef all over with salt and pepper.

5 Fry the beef in hot oil on all sides in a flameproof casserole, then remove and set aside.

6 Fry the bacon in the remaining oil, add the onion and the vegetables and sauté until browned.

7 Add the crushed allspice berries and the peppercorns as well as the bay leaves and pour in some of the beef broth (stock). Put the beef on top of the vegetables, cover and braise for about 2–2½ hours over a low heat until tender.

8 Keep adding some of the beef broth (stock) and turning the beef every so often.

9 Season to taste with salt and pepper and serve.

LAMB STEW WITH SAFFRON

Ingredients

2¼ lb / 1 kg lamb (from the shoulder)

2 onions

2 cloves garlic

2 tbsp. oil

2 cups / 500 ml lamb broth (stock)

1 lb / 450 g sweet potatoes

14 oz / 400 g can chickpeas

a few saffron threads

1 cinnamon stick

1 tbsp. honey

lemon juice

salt

cayenne pepper

fresh basil leaves, shredded, to garnish

Method
Prep and cook time: 1 h 45 min

1 Chop the lamb into bite-size pieces.

2 Peel the onions and the garlic and finely chop.

3 Fry the meat in hot oil until browned all over. Add the onions and the garlic and sauté, then pour in some of the lamb broth (stock) so that the meat is completely covered. Cover with a lid and simmer gently for about 30 minutes.

4 Meanwhile, peel the sweet potatoes and cut into cubes.

5 Drain and rinse the chickpeas and add to the meat, together with the potatoes, cinnamon, honey and saffron threads. Simmer for a further 60 minutes over a low heat. Stir occasionally, adding a little lamb broth (stock) if necessary.

6 Season to taste with lemon juice, salt and cayenne pepper, sprinkle shredded basil leaves over the top and serve.

BAKED FISH
WITH VEGETABLES

Ingredients

1lb 12 oz / 800 g white fish fillets,
such as sole or monkfish

6 bell peppers, red, yellow and green

4 shallots

2 cloves garlic

2 balls of mozzarella cheese

3 tbsp. olive oil

1 tbsp. tomato paste (purée)

1 cup / 250 ml white wine

paprika, sweet

sea salt & milled pepper

some fresh thyme leaves and sprigs

cayenne pepper

Method
Prep and cook time: 45 min

1 Heat the oven to 350°F (180°C / gas mark 4).

2 Cut the fish into large even-sized pieces.

3 De-seed the bell peppers and chop into thin slices. Peel and finely chop the shallots and the garlic. Slice the mozzarella.

4 Sauté the shallots, garlic and the bell peppers in hot oil in a flameproof oven dish. Add the tomato purée and pour in the white wine.

5 Remove from the heat and put the fish fillets on the top. Season with paprika, sea salt and pepper and cover with sliced mozzarella. Sprinkle a few thyme leaves over the top.

6 Bake in the oven until cooked (about 20 minutes). Add a little water if needed.

7 Season to taste with sea salt and pepper, sprinkle the remaining thyme sprigs over the top and serve.

BEEF GOULASH

Ingredients

2 lb / about 1 kg beef chuck, cubed

3 tbsp. oil

4 onions

2 cloves garlic

1 tbsp. paprika, sweet

½ tsp. caraway seeds, ground

2 cups / 500 ml beef broth (stock)

salt & freshly milled pepper

1 bay leaf

1 tsp. paprika, hot

1 tbsp. marjoram leaves, fresh

Method

Prep and cook time: 1 h 45 min

1 Fry the beef on all sides in hot oil, a few pieces at a time, until browned.

2 Peel the onion and the garlic. Cut the onions in half, then into slices. Chop the garlic.

3 Reduce the heat and sauté the onions together with the meat.

4 Add the sweet paprika and the ground caraway, then pour in the beef broth (stock). Now add the bay leaf, the garlic and the hot paprika.

5 Simmer over a low heat for about 1–1½ hours, stirring occasionally. Add a little water if necessary.

6 When cooked, season to taste with salt and pepper and sprinkle a few marjoram leaves over the top. Serve with bread or boiled potatoes

CHICKPEA AND BEAN DAL WITH CARAWAY POTATOES

Ingredients

2¼ cups / 400 g chickpeas, dried

2¼ cups / 400 g fava (broad) beans, dried

2 cloves garlic

2 onions

2 green chilies

2 tbsp. / 25 g clarified butter or oil

3 cups / 800 ml vegetable broth (stock)

1 tsp. freshly grated ginger

½ tsp coriander seeds, crushed

1¾ lb / 800 g potatoes

1 tsp. caraway seeds

1 handful spinach leaves

salt & freshly milled pepper

Method

Prep and cook time: 1 h 10 min, plus soaking time: 12h

1 Soak the chickpeas and the fava (broad) beans in water overnight, then drain.

2 Peel and finely chop the garlic and the onion. Cut the chilies in half.

3 Sauté the onions and garlic in hot clarified butter or oil in a saucepan, then pour in the vegetable broth (stock).

4 Add the chickpeas, fava beans, chilies, ginger, and crushed coriander seeds. Cover and simmer gently over a low heat for 50–60 minutes.

5 Peel the potatoes and boil in salted water, together with the caraway seeds for about 25 minutes until cooked.

6 Wash the spinach and add to the dal at the last moment. Season with salt and pepper.

7 Drain the potatoes and arrange onto plates. Add a spoonful of dal and serve.

BEEF RAGOUT WITH OLIVES

Ingredients

1¾ lb / 800 g lean beef, diced

5 tbsp. olive oil

salt & freshly milled pepper

2 onions, peeled and finely chopped

3 cloves garlic, peeled and finely chopped

3 carrots, peeled and cut into pieces

2 stalks celery, finely chopped

¾—1 cup / 200 ml red wine

1 bunch fresh basil leaves

2 cups / 500 ml beef broth (stock)

2 cans peeled tomatoes (1¾ lb / 800 g altogether)

2 tsp. sugar

6 tbsp. green olives, pitted

Method

Prep and cook time: 1 h 15 min

1 Heat 5 tablespoons olive oil in a stew pan and brown the meat on all sides over a fairly high heat. Season with salt and pepper.

2 Add the onions, garlic, celery and carrots and fry briefly. Then add half of the red wine and boil until completely reduced.

3 Add the rest of the red wine and reduce again.

4 Now add the beef broth (stock), tomatoes, a handful of basil leaves (reserve some for garnish) and 2 teaspoons sugar, cover and cook over a low heat for 50 minutes.

5 Add the olives 10 minutes before the end of cooking time.

6 Season with salt and plenty of pepper. Stir in more fresh basil leaves and serve.

BEAN SOUP WITH PASTA

Ingredients

1 large white onion

6 tomatoes

1 stick celery, chopped

4 tbsp. olive oil

1 lb 6 oz / 600 g canned borlotti beans, drained and rinsed

some fresh basil

some fresh parsley

salt & freshly milled pepper

1 cup / 250 g macaroni or other short tubular pasta

Parmesan cheese, to serve

Method
Prep and cook time: 45 min

1 Peel and finely chop the onion. Drop the tomatoes into boiling water for a few seconds, then skin, halve, deseed and cut into small pieces. Trim and chop the celery

2 Heat 4 tablespoons oil in a pan and sauté the onion until translucent. Add the tomatoes and celery, cover and cook over a low heat for about 25 minutes.

3 Add the beans, basil and parsley and season with salt and pepper. Pour in enough water to cover the beans and vegetables and bring to the boil. Add the pasta and cook until the pasta is done, stirring frequently.

4 Season to taste with salt and pepper. Serve sprinkled with freshly grated Parmesan cheese.

BRAZILIAN SHRIMP STEW WITH COCONUT MILK

Ingredients

14 oz / 400 g frozen shrimp (or prawns), defrosted

2 carrots

7 oz / 200 g potatoes

7 oz / 200 g spinach

1 tbsp. oil

1 can chopped tomatoes (about 14 oz / 400 g)

1 can coconut milk

a pinch of sugar

salt & freshly milled pepper

2 tbsp. fish sauce

red curry powder, to taste

2 scallion (spring onion)

1 tbsp. / 15 g butter

Method
Prep and cook time: 25 min

1 Peel and grate the carrots and potatoes. Wash and chop the spinach.

2 Heat the oil and sauté the potatoes and carrots. Add the chopped tomatoes and simmer for about 10 minutes, stirring occasionally.

3 Add the coconut milk and season with sugar, salt, pepper, fish sauce and curry powder.

4 Cut the green part of the scallion (spring onion) into rings and finely dice the rest.

5 Heat the butter in a skillet and sauté the diced scallion with the shrimp. Add to the stew. Add the spinach, return to a boil and check the seasoning, adding more if necessary.

6 Ladle into bowls and serve garnished with the scallion rings.

CHICKEN AND CHORIZO CHILI

Ingredients

2 chicken breasts

2 slices bacon

3½ oz / 100 g chorizo, Spanish spiced pork sausage

1 can kidney beans (about 14 oz / 400 g)

1 can cannellini beans (about 14 oz / 400 g)

2 red onions

2 cloves garlic

1 tbsp. olive oil

1 tbsp. tomato paste (purée)

1¾ cups / 400 ml meat broth (stock)

1 tbsp. paprika, noble sweet

salt & freshly milled pepper

cayenne pepper

pinch of dried oregano

4 tbsp. sour cream

Method

Prep and cook time: 1 h

1 Thinly slice the chicken breasts. Cut the bacon into strips. Thinly slice the chorizo.

2 Rinse and drain the beans. Peel and dice the onions and garlic.

3 Heat the oil and sauté the chicken, bacon and chorizo. Add the garlic and half of the onions and stir in the tomato paste (purée).

4 Stir in a little broth (stock). Add the paprika and simmer for about 20 minutes, stirring occasionally. Keep adding a little more broth (stock).

5 Then add the beans and simmer for a further 20 minutes or so. Season to taste with salt, pepper and cayenne pepper.

6 Spoon into bowls, scatter with the rest of the onion and sprinkle with a little oregano. Add a spoonful of sour cream to each serving.
Serve with tortilla.

TOAD IN THE HOLE (SAUSAGES IN BATTER)

Ingredients

6–10 fresh pork sausages

1 cup / 125 g flour

½ tsp. baking powder

½ tsp. salt

2 large eggs

1¼ cups / 300 ml milk

3 tbsp. / 40 g lard or oil

2 tbsp. finely chopped parsley

Method

Prep and cook time: 1 h plus
standing time: 20 min

1 Preheat the oven to 400°F (200°C / gas mark 6). For the Yorkshire pudding batter, put the flour, baking powder and salt into a mixing bowl. Add the eggs and milk and mix well. Leave to stand for 20 minutes.

2 Put the lard (or oil) into a roasting dish and put into the oven. Prick the sausages several times, put into the hot fat and roast in the oven until lightly browned.

3 Take the sausages out of the dish, pour in the batter and lay the sausages in the batter. Sprinkle with parsley and bake in the oven for 30–40 minutes.

4 The Yorkshire pudding should be light, crisp and well risen.

LANCASHIRE HOTPOT

Ingredients

1¼ lb / 500 g lamb (from the neck)

1 onion

2 carrots

1 stick of celery

1 lb 6 oz / 600 g potatoes

1½ tbsp. / 20 g butter

marjoram

sea salt & freshly milled pepper

3 cups / 750 ml broth (stock)

Method

Prep and cook time: 1 h 45 min

1 Preheat the oven to 400°F (200°C / gas mark 6). Wash the meat, pat dry with paper towel and cut into smallish cubes.

2 Wash, trim, peel and finely dice the vegetables (apart from the potatoes).

3 Peel the potatoes and slice thinly, using a mandolin vegetable slicer, if available.

4 Butter a casserole dish and put all the ingredients into it in layers, beginning with a layer of potatoes, then marjoram and seasoning, vegetables and meat. Finish with a neat layer of potatoes and season again.

5 Pour the broth (stock) over, cover and cook in the oven for about 90 minutes. Shortly before the end of cooking time remove the lid to brown the potatoes.

CHEESE-STUFFED TOMATOES

Ingredients

4 large tomatoes

salt & freshly milled pepper

3 tbsp. olive oil

1 slice white bread, diced

1 tsp. chopped rosemary

1 tsp. chopped parsley

5–7 oz / 150–200 g sheep's cheese

Method

Prep and cook time: 40 min

1 Preheat the oven to 200°C (400°F / gas mark 6). Cut out a lid from each tomato. Hollow out the tomatoes and season inside with salt. Turn over and stand on paper towel to draw out some of the water.

2 Heat 2 tablespoons oil and fry the diced bread. Add the herbs, season with salt and pepper and leave to cool. Then mix with the crumbled sheep's cheese.

3 Fill the tomatoes with the stuffing and put into a baking dish greased with 1 teaspoon oil. Put the lids on the tomatoes.

4 Sprinkle with the remaining oil and bake for about 25 minutes.

CHICKEN STEW WITH CHANTERELLES

Ingredients

1 chicken, jointed (legs, wings, breast)

2 large scallions (spring onions)

14 oz / 400 g baking potatoes

2 carrots

2 parsnips

salt & freshly milled pepper

2 tbsp. olive oil

2 cloves garlic, peeled

1¼ cups / 300 ml chicken broth (stock)

1 bay leaf

7 oz / 200 g chanterelles

2 tbsp. / 25 g butter

2 tbsp. thyme leaves

a few fresh sage leaves

Method

Prep and cook time: 1 h 15 min

1 Trim the scallions (spring onions) and cut into 2 inch (5 cm) lengths.

2 Peel the potatoes and dice finely, so that they will disintegrate and thicken the sauce.

3 Peel the carrots and parsnips and quarter lengthways.

4 Season the chicken pieces with salt and pepper, heat the oil in a large pan and brown the chicken pieces on all sides. Then add the vegetables, garlic and the broth (stock).

5 Add the bay leaf, cover and stew gently for about 1 hour. Stir frequently and add more broth if necessary.

6 Clean the chanterelles and sauté in butter. Remove from the heat.

7 Five minutes before the end of cooking time add the herbs and chanterelles to the stew. Check the seasoning of the sauce and serve.

LAMB STEW WITH PEAS AND POTATOES

Ingredients

1 lb 2 oz / 500 g lamb pieces

2 tbsp. olive oil

2 tbsp. tomato paste (purée)

4 cups / 1 litre vegetable broth (stock)

1 pack of soup vegetables (including, for example, carrot, leek, celery, parsnip, turnip) – about 1lb / 450 g

8–10 shallots

1 bay leaf

salt & freshly milled pepper

1 lb / 450 g potatoes

3 carrots

a few sprigs of marjoram

1 tsp. dried savory

2½ cups / 300 g frozen peas

1 tbsp. flour

1 tbsp. / 15 g butter

Method
Prep and cook time: 1 h

1 Heat the oil in a large pan and brown the meat on all sides. Add the tomato paste (purée) and vegetable broth (stock) and bring to a boil.

2 Meanwhile prepare the soup vegetables and chop very finely. Peel the shallots and cut off the roots.

3 Skim off any scum from the meat broth (stock) with a skimmer and add the soup vegetables, shallots, bay leaf and seasoning to the meat. Cover and simmer for about 40 minutes.

4 Meanwhile peel the potatoes and carrots. Halve or quarter the potatoes and cut the carrots into ¾ inch (2 cm) lengths. Add to the meat after 10 minutes cooking time and simmer until the meat is tender.

5 Finely chop the marjoram. About 10 minutes before the end of cooking time add the marjoram, savory and frozen peas to the stew.

6 Blend the flour and butter into a paste, stir into the stew and bring to a boil. Allow to thicken slightly, then check the seasoning, remove the bay leaf and serve.

BRAISED PORK
WITH MUSHROOMS AND OLIVES

Ingredients

2¼ lbs / 1 kg pork loin

1 tbsp. flour

2 cloves garlic

3 cups / 250 g small button mushrooms

4 tbsp. olive oil

1 cup / 250 ml white wine

1¾ cups / 200 g green olives, pitted

salt & freshly milled pepper

2 tbsp. chopped parsley

Method

Prep and cook time: 30 min

1 Wash the pork, then pat dry with paper towel and cut into cubes. Sprinkle flour all over the meat.

2 Peel and finely chop the garlic. Clean the mushrooms and cut into slices.

3 Fry the mushrooms in a skillet in 2 tablespoons hot oil, then remove and set aside.

4 Heat the remaining oil in the skillet, then fry the meat on all sides until browned. Add the garlic and pour in the white wine. Add the mushrooms and the olives, then season with salt and pepper.

5 Cover with a lid and simmer on a low heat for about 10–15 minutes. Add a little water if necessary.

6 Season to taste with salt and pepper, sprinkle chopped parsley over the top and serve.

BRAISED CHICKEN WITH VEGETABLES

Ingredients

1 medium-sized chicken

1 onion

2 cloves garlic

2 sticks celery

2 carrots

1 lb / 450 g small potatoes

8 oz / 250 g broccoli florets

5 oz / 150 g snow (sugarsnap) peas

1 handful spinach leaves

2 tbsp. sunflower oil

1 can chopped tomatoes
(about 14 oz / 400 g)

1 cup / 250 ml chicken broth (stock)

Worcestershire sauce

1¼ cups / 150 g peas, frozen

2 tsp chopped thyme

salt & freshly milled pepper

Method

Prep and cook time: 1 h 30 min

1 Preheat the oven to 350°F (180°C / gas mark 4). Peel the onion and the garlic and chop. Wash and trim the celery and chop.

2 Peel the carrots and quarter lengthways. Peel the potatoes. Wash and trim the broccoli florets and the snow (sugarsnap) peas. Wash the spinach and leave to drain.

3 Fry the chicken in hot oil in a large flameproof casserole and remove.

4 Sauté the onions, garlic, celery, carrots and potatoes. Add the tomatoes and pour in the chicken broth (stock) and Worcestershire sauce.

5 Put the chicken inside the casserole, cover and cook in the oven for about 1 hour.

6 Take the chicken out of the pot and add the remaining vegetables. Cook for a further 10 minutes.

7 Remove the skin and bones from the chicken and cut into pieces. Put the chicken back in the casserole, sprinkle chopped thyme over the top and cook for a further 5 minutes. Season to taste and serve.

BUTTERNUT SQUASH AND POTATO GRATIN

Ingredients

1 clove garlic, peeled

1 lb / 450 g boiling potatoes, thinly sliced

1 lb / 450 g butternut squash, peeled, seeds removed, thinly sliced

10 sage leaves

2 cups / 500 ml light (single) cream

1 cup / 100 g grated cheese, such as Cheddar

2 tbsp. crème fraîche

salt & freshly milled pepper

grated nutmeg

Method

Prep and cook time: 1 h 15 min

1 Preheat the oven to 350°F (180°C / gas mark 4). Rub a baking dish with the garlic.

2 Layer the potato and butternut squash in an alternating pattern in the baking dish. Scatter a few sage leaves in between.

3 Mix the cream with the grated cheese and crème fraîche. Season with salt, pepper and grated nutmeg and pour over the vegetables. The vegetables should be barely covered.

4 Bake for 40–50 minutes until golden brown.

5 Test with a fork to see if the vegetables are ready.

POT AU FEU (FRENCH CHICKEN AND VEGETABLE STEW)

Ingredients

1 chicken, weighing about 2½ lbs / 1.2 kg, cut into 8 pieces

3 tbsp. olive oil

1 tbsp. thyme, dried

2 bay leaves

1 clove garlic, finely diced

1 bunch scallions (spring onions), trimmed and chopped

7 oz / 200 g small carrots

14 oz / 400 g small potatoes, scrubbed

8 oz / 250 g green asparagus, trimmed and cut into small pieces

chicken broth (stock) granules or cube

salt & freshly milled pepper

Method

Prep and cook time: 1 h

1 Season the chicken pieces well and fry on all sides in a little oil until browned.

2 Add the thyme, bay leaves and garlic. Sweat briefly with the chicken, then add sufficient cold water to cover the contents of the pan.

3 Simmer gently for 30 minutes, removing the scum from time to time.

4 Add the prepared vegetables except the asparagus and simmer for a further 15 minutes. Add the asparagus and simmer for 5 more minutes.

5 Add the broth (stock) granules and season with salt and pepper to taste.

VEAL CASSEROLE WITH MUSHROOMS AND VEGETABLES

Ingredients

1 lb 6 oz / 600 g veal

1 pack of soup vegetables (including, for example, carrot, leek, celery, parsnip, turnip) – about 1lb / 450 g

salt & white pepper

1 tbsp. peppercorns

1 tbsp. mustard seeds

2 bay leaves

14 oz / 250 g carrots

2–3 sticks celery

scant 1 cup / 200 g small button mushrooms

2 tbsp. / 25 g butter

2 tbsp. flour

½ cup / 120 ml white wine

scant ½ cup / 100 ml cream

1 tbsp. lemon juice

cilantro (coriander) or parsley leaves, to garnish

Method

Prep and cook time: 1 h 40 min

1 Put the veal into a large pan together with the prepared soup vegetables, salt, peppercorns, mustard seeds and bay leaves.

2 Add just enough water to cover the meat. Cover with a lid and simmer gently over a medium heat for 1 hour.

3 Take the meat out and leave to cool. Strain the broth (stock) through a sieve into a pan and boil until the liquid has reduced to approximately 1 cup (250 ml).

4 Peel the carrots and cut into sticks. Trim the celery and cut into pieces. Blanch both in salted water for 3 minutes, then take out and put immediately into cold water, then drain.

5 Halve or quarter the mushrooms. Cut the cooked veal into bite-size pieces.

6 Heat the butter in a pan, stir in the flour and cook until pale yellow. Now pour in the white wine, reduced meat broth (stock) and cream. Add the mushrooms, carrot sticks and celery and simmer for 5 minutes.

7 Then add the meat, season with salt and pepper and a few drops of lemon juice. Reheat the meat in the sauce for 5–10 minutes, then serve sprinkled with chopped cilantro (coriander) or parsley leaves.

BEEF RAGOUT
WITH CHANTERELLE MUSHROOMS

Ingredients

2¼ lbs / 1 kg beef chuck, chopped

3 onions

2 garlic cloves

2 tbsp. flour

2–4 tbsp sunflower oil

good ½ cup / 150 ml port wine

1 cup / 250 ml beef broth (stock)

salt & freshly milled pepper

1 bay leaf

14 oz / 400 g chanterelle mushrooms

2 tbsp. / 25 g butter

2 tbsp. chopped parsley

Method
Prep and cook time: 2 h

1 Peel and finely chop the onions and garlic.

2 Coat the meat with flour and fry in hot oil, a few pieces at a time. Remove from the pan and fry the onions and the garlic until browned.

3 Add the meat again and pour in the port wine. Pour in some of the beef broth (stock) and season with salt, pepper and the bay leaf.

4 Cover with a lid and cook on a low heat for about 1½ hours, stirring occasionally. Add a little broth if needed.

5 In the meantime clean the chanterelle mushrooms and fry in hot butter. Season with salt and pepper.

6 When the ragout is cooked, add the chanterelle mushrooms and stir. Sprinkle the chopped parsley over the top and serve.

BAKED COD AND SEAFOOD COBBLER

Ingredients

1 lb / 500 g cod fillets

2 shallots

1 clove garlic

scant 2 cups / 125 g mushrooms

1 zucchini (courgette)

2 tomatoes

2 tbsp. olive oil

scant ½ cup / 100 ml white wine

¾ cup / 200 ml fish broth (stock)

1–2 tbsp. cornstarch (cornflour)

2 tbsp. chopped parsley

5 oz / 150 g shrimp or prawns), ready to cook

salt & freshly milled pepper

For the topping:

2½ cups / 250 g flour

3 tsp. baking powder

½ tsp. salt

¼ cup / 50 g soft butter

2/3 cup / 150 ml milk

flour, for rolling out

¼ cup / 25 g grated cheese

Method

Prep and cook time: 1 h 30 min

1 Preheat the oven to 400°F (200°C / gas mark 6).

2 Cut the fish into pieces. Peel and finely chop the shallots and the garlic.

3 Chop the mushrooms. Trim and slice the zucchini (courgette). Quarter, de-seed the tomatoes and cut into cubes.

4 Sauté the shallots and the garlic in hot oil. Add the mushrooms, zucchini and tomatoes, then pour in the white wine and the fish broth (stock). Bring to a boil.

5 Mix the cornstarch (cornflour) to a paste with a little water, then add to the sauce, stirring continually until the sauce is rich and creamy.

6 Remove from the heat and add the chopped parsley, fish and prawns. Season to taste with salt and pepper and pour into a baking dish.

7 For the topping, mix the flour with the baking powder, salt, butter and enough milk to bind, and knead until the dough is soft.

8 Roll out on a floured surface to about ½ inch (1½ cm) thick. Use a 1½ inch (3 cm) cookie cutter to cut the dough into rounds.

9 Brush with milk, then put on the fish. Sprinkle with cheese and bake the oven for about 30 minutes until golden brown.

IRISH STEW WITH SAVOY CABBAGE

Ingredients

1 lb 12 oz / 800 g lamb, from the leg

1 small Savoy cabbage

14 oz / 400 g potatoes

1 leek

2 carrots

2 onions

2 cloves garlic

salt & freshly milled pepper

1 pinch caraway seeds, ground

1 bunch flat-leaf parsley

1 bay leaf

3½ cups / 900 ml beef broth (stock)

Grated zest of ½ lemon

Method

Prep and cook time: 2 h 30 min

1 Pre-heat the oven to 325°F (170°C / gas mark 3).

2 Cut the fat off the meat and cut into about 1 inch (3 cm) cubes. Quarter the Savoy cabbage, remove the core and roughly shred. Scrub the potatoes and cut into dice.

3 Cut the leek diagonally into slices. Peel the carrots and cut into slices. Peel and finely chop the onions and the garlic.

4 Put a layer of Savoy cabbage on the bottom of a casserole, followed by some lamb, onions and garlic. Season with salt, pepper and ground caraway.

5 Add a layer of potatoes, leek and carrots and season again. Carry on layering the casserole until all ingredients have been used up. Finish with a layer of vegetables.

6 Put half the parsley and the bay leaf on the top. Pour in the broth (stock), cover and put on the lower shelf of the oven

7 Cook for about 1½ hours, then open the lid and remove the bay leaf and the parsley. Cook for a further 30 minutes without the lid.

8 Adjust the seasoning, sprinkle the remaining chopped parsley and lemon zest over the top and serve.

CHORIZO STEW WITH CRÈME FRAÎCHE

Ingredients

8 oz / 250 g chorizo, Spanish spiced pork sausage

2 onions

1–2 cloves garlic

14 oz / 400 g potatoes

1 pack of soup vegetables (including, for example, leek, celery, parsnip, swede) – about 1lb / 450 g

2 carrots

3 tbsp. olive oil

1 can tomatoes (about 14 oz / 400 g)

2 cups / 500 ml vegetable broth (stock)

salt & freshly milled pepper

1 bay leaf

1–2 tsp. oregano, dried

1¹/₃ cups / 200 g chickpeas, canned, drained

a small tub of crème fraîche

fresh parsley, to garnish

Method

Prep and cook time: 50 min

1 Peel the onions and the garlic. Cut the onion in half, then into small wedges. Chop the garlic. Peel the chorizo sausage and cut into slices.

2 Peel the potatoes and cut into cubes. Peel the soup vegetables and chop into small chunks. Peel the carrots and cut into rings.

3 Fry the chorizo sausage in a little oil in a flameproof casserole, then add the onions and the garlic and sauté until soft.

4 Add the potatoes, soup vegetables, carrots, tomatoes and pour in the vegetable broth (stock). Season with salt, pepper, bay leaf and oregano.

5 Cover with a lid and simmer gently for about 30 minutes on a low heat.

6 Rinse the chickpeas, then add to the soup and heat. Season with salt and pepper and serve with a spoonful of crème fraîche and fresh parsley.

PAELLA

Ingredients

2 tomatoes

9 oz / 250 g shrimp (prawns), peeled and ready to cook

1 lb 12 oz / 800 g shellfish, (e.g. mussels)

6 tbsp. olive oil

About 2 lb / 1 kg of mixed skinless and boneless chicken

1 onion, finely diced

1 clove garlic, finely diced

2 red bell peppers, cut into strips

scant 1 cup / 100 g frozen peas

salt & freshly milled pepper

1 cup / 200 g paella rice

1¾ cups / 400 ml chicken broth (stock)

1 bay leaf

4 saffron threads

Method
Prep and cook time: 1 h

1 Drop the tomatoes into boiling water for a few seconds, then skin, quarter, de-seed and chop.

2 Wash the shrimp (prawns), scrub the shellfish, scrape off the 'beards' from the mussels. Discard any shells that do not close when tapped.

3 Heat the oil in a large skillet or paella pan and slowly sauté the chicken on all sides until golden brown. Add the onion and fry briefly. Add the chopped garlic, bell peppers, tomatoes and peas and fry briefly. Season with salt and pepper.

4 Scatter the rice into the skillet and stir in carefully. Add the broth (stock), bay leaf and the saffron dissolved in a little water. You should not stir the paella again. Turn down the heat and simmer without a lid for 25–30 minutes.

5 About 10 minutes before the end of cooking time add the seafood. When cooked, discard any shells that remain closed. Check the seasoning and serve. The liquid should have been absorbed.

SPICY LAMB WITH PAPRIKA

Ingredients

1¾ lb / 800 g lamb

4 onions

2 tbsp. flour

4 tbsp. sunflower oil

1 tbsp. tomato paste (purée)

2 cups / 500 ml lamb broth (stock)

7 oz / 200 g canned chopped tomatoes

1 tbsp. paprika, sweet

1 tbsp. paprika, hot

1 tsp. caraway seeds

salt and cayenne pepper

parsley sprig, to garnish

Method

Prep and cook time: 2 h 15 min

1 Peel and dice the onions.

2 Cut the meat into bite-size cubes and sprinkle all over with a little flour.

3 Heat the oil in a skillet and brown the meat on all sides over a fairly high heat, a few pieces at a time. When the meat has browned, take it out of the skillet and sweat the onions.

4 Then stir in the tomato paste (purée) and return the meat to the skillet. Pour in the broth (stock), tomatoes and spices and bring to a boil.

5 Simmer over a low heat for 1½–2 hours, stirring from time to time. Add a little more broth if necessary. Season well with salt and cayenne pepper and serve garnished with parsley.

SPICY CLAM, PORK AND TOMATO STEW

Ingredients

14 oz / 400 g pork

14 oz / 400 g clams

14 oz / 400 g onions

salt & freshly milled pepper

4 tbsp. olive oil

2 tbsp. tomato paste (purée)

1 tbsp. paprika, noble sweet

1 tsp. paprika, hot

¾ cup / 200 ml fish broth (stock)

1 beefsteak tomato, skinned, de-seeded and diced

1 clove garlic

scant ½ cup / 100 ml white wine

fresh basil leaves, shredded

Method

Prep and cook time: 1 h 20 min, plus 2–3 h soaking time

1 Put the clams in salted cold water for two to three hours and shake occasionally to remove any sand. Discard any that do not close when tapped. Scrub the remainder.

2 Peel and finely dice the onions.

3 Cut the meat into bite-size pieces and season with salt and pepper. Heat half of the oil and quickly brown the meat on all sides over a fairly high heat, then take out of the pan. (You may need to do this in batches).

4 Then sauté the onions in the frying fat. Return the meat to the pan, stir in the tomato paste (purée) and season with paprika. Sauté briefly, stirring, then add the fish broth (stock) and bring to a boil.

5 Cover and simmer for about 1 hour, stirring from time to time. Add the diced tomato about half-way through cooking time.

6 Peel and finely chop the garlic. Heat the remaining oil in a skillet and brown the garlic. Add the clams and sauté over a low heat, until the clams open. Discard any that remain closed. Add the wine and briefly bring to a boil.

7 When the meat stew is cooked mix in the clams and check the seasoning. Add the finely shredded basil and serve.

CHILI BEEF WITH WINTER VEGETABLES

Ingredients

1 lb 6 oz / 600 g beef, for stewing (such as from the leg)

1 lb 6 oz / 600 g baking potatoes

1¹/₃ cups / 200 g chickpeas, canned, drained

2 onions

2 cloves garlic

5 tomatoes

3–4 tbsp. sunflower oil

a pinch of curry powder

¼ tsp. cayenne pepper

½ tsp. ground cumin

1¾ cups / 400 ml meat broth (stock)

1¾ cups / 200 g frozen peas

salt

2 tbsp. pumpkin seeds

Method

Prep and cook time: 1 h 30 min

1 Cut the beef into cubes. Peel and roughly dice the potatoes. Rinse the chickpeas.

2 Peel and chop the onions and garlic. Drop the tomatoes into boiling water for a few seconds, refresh in cold water, then skin, quarter, de-seed and dice.

3 Heat the oil and brown the meat on all sides. Add the onions and garlic and fry briefly, then add the curry powder, cayenne pepper and cumin. Add the broth (stock), cover and stew for about 30 minutes.

4 Add the potatoes, tomatoes, chickpeas and peas and simmer gently for a further 40–50 minutes. Stir occasionally and add more broth if necessary. Season to taste.

5 Toast the pumpkin seeds in a dry skillet. Serve scattered with pumpkin seeds.

SHRIMP CREOLE

Ingredients

14 oz / 400 g Andouille (Cajun smoked pork sausage)

14 oz / 400 g onions

4 cloves garlic

2 bell peppers, red and green

1 lb 2 oz / 500 g tomatoes

1 cup / 200 g long-grain rice

7 oz / 200 g okra

4 tbsp. sunflower oil

1 tsp. cayenne pepper

1 tsp. rose paprika

5 crushed allspice berries

2 bay leaves

2½ cups / 600 ml beef broth (stock)

7 oz / 200 g shrimp (prawns), peeled and ready to cook

½ bunch scallions (spring onions)

Tabasco sauce

Method
Prep and cook time: 1 h

1 Dice the sausage. Peel and roughly chop the onions. Peel and finely chop the garlic.

2 Halve, core and dice the bell peppers.

3 Drop the tomatoes into boiling water for a few seconds, refresh in cold water, then skin, quarter, de-seed and dice.

4 Cook the rice in salted water according to the package instructions.

5 Trim the okra and cut into pieces.

6 Heat the oil in a large pan and sauté the onions and garlic until translucent.

7 Add the sausage and sauté briefly, then add the bell peppers, okra, spices, bay leaves and broth (stock). Bring to a boil, cover and cook for about 12 minutes.

8 Then add the rice, shrimp (prawns), tomatoes and scallions (spring onions) and cook gently for a further 5 minutes. Season to taste with salt and Tabasco and serve.

CHUNKY THREE BEAN CHILI

Ingredients

1¾ lb / 800 g beef, from the leg

2 cloves garlic

2 chilies

1 bunch scallions (spring onions)

3 tbsp. sunflower oil

1 tbsp. tomato paste (purée)

2 tbsp. flour

2 cups / 500 ml meat broth (stock)

14 oz / 400 g canned beans, a mix of red, white and black if possible

1 tbsp. paprika, hot

cayenne pepper

salt

Method
Prep and cook time: 2 h

1 Chop the beef into bite size pieces. Peel and finely chop the garlic. Finely chop the chilies.

2 Trim the scallions (spring onions), shred the green parts and put in cold water. Slice the white parts at an angle.

3 Heat the oil and brown the meat on all sides. Add the garlic and tomato paste (purée), dust with flour and stir in the broth (stock).

4 Drain and rinse the beans. Add the beans, paprika and chilies and simmer for about 1½ hours. Add more liquid if necessary and stir occasionally.

5 Add the scallion rings for the last 30 minutes. Season with salt and cayenne pepper and serve garnished with the shredded scallions.

SAFFRON RISOTTO WITH GREEN ASPARAGUS

Ingredients

1 lb 2 oz / 500 g green asparagus

1 onion

2 tbsp. / 25 g butter

2 tbsp. olive oil

2 cups / 400 g short-grain (risotto) rice

5 saffron threads

salt & freshly milled pepper

4 cups / 1 liter vegetable broth (stock), simmering

½ cup / 80 g grated Parmesan cheese

3 tbsp. / 40 g butter

Method

Prep and cook time: 40 min

1 Clean the asparagus, remove the woody ends and cook in plenty of boiling, salted water until just tender.

2 Peel and finely chop the onion. Heat the butter and olive oil and sauté the onion until translucent.

3 Add the rice and stir over the heat until the rice looks translucent. Add 3 saffron threads and season with salt and pepper.

4 Add two ladlefuls of boiling broth (stock), stirring constantly until the stock has been absorbed. Gradually add the stock, a ladleful at a time, stirring until the stock is absorbed and the rice is tender but still has a bite in the center (18–20 minutes).

5 Stir in the Parmesan cheese and butter. Cut the asparagus into pieces and stir in carefully.

6 Spoon the risotto into dishes, sprinkle with the reserved saffron, season with pepper and serve.

POTATO GOULASH WITH SAUERKRAUT

Ingredients

2¼ lb / 1 kg baking potatoes

3 red bell peppers

1 large onion

2 sprigs fresh sage

2 tbsp. neutral oil

8 oz / 250 g sauerkraut

2 tbsp. tomato paste (purée)

1⅓ cups / 330 ml tomato juice

1 cup / 250 ml vegetable broth (stock)

salt & freshly milled pepper

1 small tub of sour cream

Method

Prep and cook time: 45 min

1 Peel the potatoes and cut into sticks about ¾ inch (2 cm) thick. Halve and core the bell peppers and cut into thin strips.

2 Peel the onion and slice very thinly. Roughly shred the sage leaves.

3 Heat the oil in a large pan and sauté the onion until translucent. Add the potatoes, bell peppers, sauerkraut, tomato paste (purée) and sage and fry for 5 minutes.

4 Add the tomato juice and vegetable broth (stock). Season with salt and pepper, cover and simmer for 20–25 minutes.

5 Then cook the goulash without a lid for a little while to reduce it slightly. Serve with a spoonful of sour cream.

BOILED BEEF
WITH VEGETABLES

Ingredients

2¼ lbs / 1 kg beef (such as chuckor brisket)

about 1 lb / 500 g meaty beef bones

1 bay leaf

3 sprigs parsley

5 sprigs marjoram

4 carrots

1 leek

2 stalks celery

1 onion

6 cloves

salt & freshly milled pepper

Method

Prep and cook time: 2 h 20 min

1 Bring about 12 cups (2½ litres) water to a boil in a large pan. Place the beef and the bones in the pan (make sure that everything is covered with water).

2 Add the bay leaf, 4 sprigs marjoram and the parsley, then reduce the heat and simmer for 1½–2 hours. Remove any scum.

3 In the meantime peel the carrots, trim the leek and celery and roughly chop. Peel the onion and press the cloves into it.

4 Place the prepared vegetables into the pan about 40 minutes towards the end of cooking time.

5 Remove the bones and take the meat out of the pan. Cut the meat into slices and place back into the pan. Season to taste with salt and pepper and serve garnished with marjoram.

CASSOULET
WITH KNUCKLE
OF PORK

Ingredients

1 small knuckle of pork

1½ cups / 300 g cannellini beans, dried

2 onions

2 cloves

1 bay leaf

2 cloves garlic

2 carrots

4 scallions (spring onions)

2 sprigs rosemary

½ cup / 100 g black olives, pitted

salt & freshly milled pepper

Method

Prep and cook time: 2 h, plus 12 hours soaking time

1 Soak the beans overnight. Drain the beans.

2 Peel an onion and press the cloves and the bay leaf into it.

3 Put the onion together with the beans and the pork in a large pan, cover with water and simmer for about 1½ hours. Add water if needed and remove any scum.

4 In the meantime, peel the garlic, carrots and the onion and roughly chop. Trim the scallions (spring onions) and cut into pieces.

5 About 30 minutes before the end of cooking time, put the vegetables, the rosemary and the olives in the pan.

6 At the end of cooking time (when the beans are cooked), take the pork out of the pan, remove the bone and cut the meat into cubes. Remove the onion clove.

7 Put the pork back into the pan and season to taste with salt and pepper.

POT-AU-FEU
WITH BELLY PORK

Ingredients

3 lb 4 oz / 1½ kg pork belly, with thin layer of fat but no skin

sea salt & freshly milled pepper

6 fresh sage leaves

2 tbsp. sunflower oil

2 stalks celery

2 leeks

6 cloves garlic

3 carrots

4 large potatoes, boiling

½ small Savoy cabbage

2 bay leaves

6 sprigs thyme

2 sprigs sage

1 sprig rosemary

1 sprig marjoram

4 shallots

1 handful of parsley leaves, chopped

Method
Prep and cook time: 3 h

1 Season the meat with salt and pepper, place the sage leaves on the top and roll up tight. Fasten with kitchen twine.

2 Fry the meat in hot oil on all sides. Place in a large pan and pour in about 15 cups (3 liters) water. Add 1 teaspoon salt and bring to a boil. Simmer for 1 hour, scooping off any scum.

3 In the meantime trim the vegetables and tie the herbs together. Chop the celery and the leek into 3 inch (7 cm) pieces. Peel and chop the garlic.

4 Peel the carrots, cut in half lengthways, then into quarters. Peel the potatoes and roughly chop. Cut the Savoy cabbage into 4–6 wedges.

5 At the end of the hour, add the carrots, the herb bouquet and the garlic and simmer for another 30 minutes.

6 Now add the rest of the ingredients, apart from the parsley, and simmer for 1 hour.

7 Take the meat out of the soup and remove the kitchen twine. Cut into slices and place into bowls. Spoon some of the soup and vegetables over the top, garnish with parsley and serve.

BAKED STUFFED MUSHROOMS
WITH BACON AND CHEESE TOPPING

Ingredients

12 large mushrooms

4 oz / 125 g chanterelle mushrooms

1 clove garlic

3 scallions (spring onions)

1 tbsp butter

2 slices (rashers) bacon

1 tbsp. chopped parsley

2 tsp. chopped marjoram

salt & freshly milled pepper

2 dashes Worcestershire sauce

½ cup / 60 g grated cheese, (such as Gruyère)

scant ½ cup / 100 ml vegetable broth (stock)

4 tbsp. croutons

rosemary, to garnish

Method

Prep and cook time: 45 min

1 Pre-heat the oven to 400°F (200°C / gas mark 6).

2 Clean the large mushrooms, remove the stems and scrape out some of the center. Chop the stems. Clean the chanterelle mushrooms and chop.

3 Peel the garlic and finely chop. Slice the scallions (spring onions) into rings.

4 Sauté the scallions (spring onions) in hot butter until soft, then add the garlic and the chopped mushrooms. Leave for about 3 minutes on a high heat to extract the juices.

5 Finely chop the bacon. Take the skillet off the heat and let the mushrooms cool.

6 Now add the chopped herbs and the bacon. Season with salt, pepper and Worcestershire sauce.

7 Put the large mushrooms in a buttered baking dish with the opening facing upwards. Fill the mushrooms with the mushroom mix and sprinkle grated cheese over the top.

8 Pour in the vegetable broth (stock) and bake in the oven for about 25 minutes.

9 Sprinkle croutons over the top, garnish with rosemary and serve.

JALFREZI (ANGLO-INDIAN CURRY)

Ingredients

about 1 lb / 500 g roasted meat, beef or lamb (leftover meat is ideal)

3 onions

3 tomatoes

3 green chilies

3 tbsp. sunflower oil

¼ tsp. mustard seeds

¼ tsp. cumin seeds

¼ tsp. coriander, ground

¼ tsp. turmeric, ground

1 tbsp. Worcestershire sauce

salt & freshly milled pepper

parsley, to garnish

Method

Prep and cook time: 20 min

1 Cut the meat into thin strips. Peel the onions, cut in half, then into thin slices.

2 Put the tomatoes in boiling water for a few seconds, then immediately into cold water. Skin, quarter, de-seed the tomatoes and finely chop.

3 Cut the chilies in half lengthways, de-seed and finely chop.

4 Heat the oil in a skillet and toast the mustard and cumin seeds for about 30 seconds, stirring continually.

5 Add the onions and the chilies and fry until slightly browned, stirring continually.

6 Add the meat, the ground spices, the Worcestershire sauce and the tomatoes. Season with salt and pepper and cook on a medium heat for about 3–5 minutes, stirring continuously.

7 Garnish with parsley and serve with rice.

FISH STEW
WITH CRÈME FRAÎCHE

Ingredients

1 lb 6 oz / 600 g fish fillet, such as bass or monkfish

2 carrots

1 clove garlic

2 shallots

1 bunch scallions (spring onions)

2 tbsp. / 25 g butter

1 tbsp. flour

¾–1 cup / 200 ml white wine

¾–1 cup / 200 ml fish broth (stock)

good ½ cup / 125 g crème fraîche

1 bunch dill weed

2 tsp. Noilly Prat

lemon juice

salt & white pepper

Method

Prep and cook time: 30 min

1 Dice the fish fillet.

2 Peel the carrots, garlic and shallots. Slice the carrots and finely dice the garlic and shallots. Trim the scallions (spring onions) and cut into 1 inch (3 cm) lengths.

3 Heat the butter in a frying pan and sauté the carrots, garlic and shallots. Dust with flour and stir in the white wine. Simmer until reduced slightly, then add the fish broth (stock).

4 Stir in the crème fraîche and simmer gently for 5–6 minutes. Then add the fish and scallions and cook over a low heat for a further 6–8 minutes, until done.

5 Chop the dill weed (reserving a few sprigs to garnish) and mix into the stew.

6 Season to taste with a few drops of lemon juice, Noilly Prat, salt and pepper and serve garnished with the reserved dill weed.

BEEF AND VEGETABLE STEW

Ingredients

1lb 2 oz / 500 g beef, for braising

(such as chuck)

2 chicory heads (endives)

2 carrots

1 zucchini (courgette)

8 oz / 250 g celery root (celeriac)

2 onions

2 cloves garlic

3 tbsp. sunflower oil

1¾ cups / 400 ml beef broth (stock)

7 oz / 200 g broccoli florets

salt & freshly milled pepper

1 tbsp. chopped parsley

fresh sage leaves, to garnish

Method

Prep and cook time: 1 h 20 min

1 Cut the beef into cubes.

2 Trim the chicory (endives), then cut into wedges. Peel the carrots and cut into short lengths. Trim and chop the zucchini (courgette).

3 Peel the celery root and roughly chop. Peel the onions and the garlic and finely chop.

4 Fry the meat in hot oil until browned on all sides. Add the onions and the garlic and fry until lightly browned.

5 Now add the carrots, endives, celery root (celeriac) and sauté the vegetables.

6 Pour in the broth (stock), bring to a boil, cover and simmer for about 30 minutes. Now add the broccoli florets and the zucchini and simmer for a further 30 minutes until cooked.

7 Season to taste with salt and pepper, sprinkle chopped parsley over the top, garnish with sage leaves and serve.

LAMB STEW WITH DUMPLINGS

Ingredients

1 lb 6 oz / 600 g lamb, for braising

2 onions

2 cloves garlic

2 stalks celery

7 oz / 200 g potatoes, boiling

7 oz / 200 g sweet potatoes

2 carrots

2 tbsp. sunflower oil

2¼ cups / 600 ml beef broth (stock)

salt & freshly milled pepper

2 bay leaves

For the dumplings:

2 cups / 200 g all-purpose (plain) flour

1 egg

1 tbsp. thyme leaves, dried

scant ½ cup / 100 ml milk

grated nutmeg

Method

Prep and cook time: 1 h 20 min

1 Cut the lamb into cubes.

2 Peel the onions and the garlic and chop. Trim the celery, then chop.

3 Peel the potatoes and sweet potatoes, then cut into cubes. Peel the carrots, cut in half lengthways, then chop.

4 Fry the meat in hot oil until browned on all sides. Add the onions and the garlic and pour in the broth (stock). Season and bring to a boil then simmer for about 30 minutes.

5 Add all the vegetables and bay leaves and simmer for a further 45 minutes.

6 In the meantime make the dumplings. Mix the flour, egg and thyme and add enough milk to form a dough.

7 Season with salt and freshly grated nutmeg. Use a teaspoon to form tiny balls, then place in boiling, salted water and simmer for about 10 minutes.

8 Season the stew with salt and pepper and serve with a few dumplings.

Published by Transatlantic Press

First published in 2010

Transatlantic Press
38 Copthorne Road, Croxley Green, Hertfordshire WD3 4AQ

© Transatlantic Press

Images and Recipes by StockFood © The Food Image Agency

Recipes selected by Marika Kucerova, StockFood

A catalogue record for this book is available from the British Library.

ISBN 978-1-907176-39-5

Printed in China